# A WEEKEND WITH LEONARDO DA VINCI

# A WEEKEND WITH
# LEONARDO DA VINCI

Text by Rosabianca Skira-Venturi
translated by Ann Keay Beneduce

RIZZOLI
NEW YORK

First published in the United States of America in 1993 by
Rizzoli International Publications, Inc.
300 Park Avenue South, New York, New York 10010

Series under the direction of R. Skira and Y.-M. Maquet
Copyright © 1992 by Editions d'Art Albert Skira S. A., Geneva
English edition copyright © 1993 by Rizzoli International Publications, Inc.

Library of Congress Cataloging-in-Publication Data

Skira-Venturi, Rosabianca.
    {Dimanche avec Leonardo da Vinci. English}
    A weekend with Leonardo da Vinci / text by Rosabianca Skira-Venturi
and Yves-Marie Maquet ; translated by Ann Beneduce.
        p.  cm.
    Summary: The fifteenth-century artist talks about his life and work as if
entertaining the reader for a weekend.
    ISBN 0-8478-1440-8
    1. Leonardo, da Vinci, 1452–1519—Juvenile literature. 2. Artists—
Italy—Biography—Juvenile literature. [1. Leonardo, Da Vinci,
1452–1519. 2. Artists.] I. Title. II. Title: Leonardo da Vinci.
    N6923.L33S5813  1993
    709'.2—dc20                                          91–12425
                                                            CIP
                                                             AC

Design by Mary McBride

Printed in Hong Kong

It's the weekend. How would you like to spend a day or two with me? Take a look at this picture of me, with my long white beard. This is how I drew myself when I was already old, in Milan, a city in Italy. Do you know my name? Well, I might as well tell you right away, I like my name because it makes me think of a lion, with his courage, nobility, and his great mane. Lion is *Leone* in Italian, and my first name is *Leonardo*. Now I'm more than sixty years old and I live in a very beautiful house in France where Francis I, the king of France, has invited me to stay. But I was born in an Italian village called Vinci and my name is

## LEONARDO DA VINCI

However, unlike the lion who, once he has had his fill, falls into a long peaceful sleep, I am never still. I am always ready to pounce on something—it may be something I see in nature, the expression on someone's face, or the movement of some animal—I want to seize some of the thousands of ideas that cross my mind and try to explain them to myself. I must confess that I rather like the way I look now, like a patriarch, which is a man who has become very wise as he has grown old. And how did I become such a wise old man? Well, I've never stopped exploring the mysteries of mankind and the universe. I wonder, can one really unravel all those mysteries? All my life I have tracked them down, asking: Why is this? What is that? What machine would do this? What other would do that? Who are we? How do we live? I have always been a very curious sort of person. And what a life I've led! People think of me first as a painter and sculptor, but I have also been an inventor and an engineer, as well as a director of plays, splendid public celebrations, grand parades, and festivals. Sometimes people ask how I was able to do all that.

*A few strokes of the artist's pen and out springs a* Roaring Lion; *in another mood, for the young* St. John the Baptist *that you see on the opposite page, da Vinci used delicate shades of charcoal with touches of soft colors.*

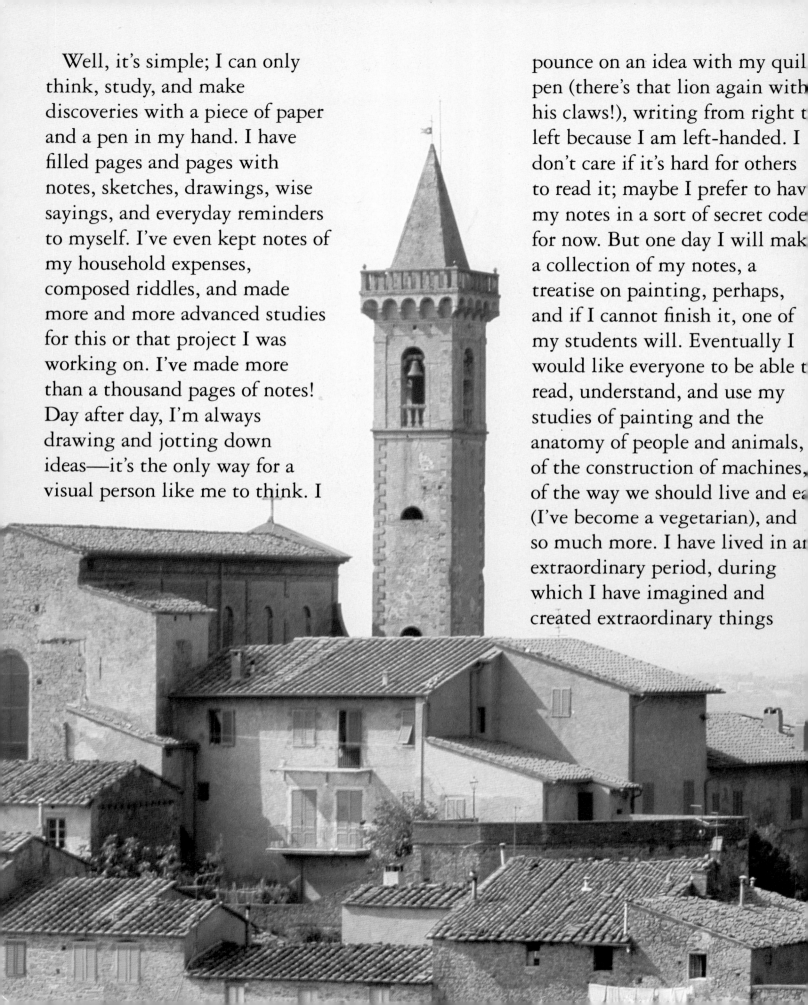

Well, it's simple; I can only think, study, and make discoveries with a piece of paper and a pen in my hand. I have filled pages and pages with notes, sketches, drawings, wise sayings, and everyday reminders to myself. I've even kept notes of my household expenses, composed riddles, and made more and more advanced studies for this or that project I was working on. I've made more than a thousand pages of notes! Day after day, I'm always drawing and jotting down ideas—it's the only way for a visual person like me to think. I pounce on an idea with my quil pen (there's that lion again with his claws!), writing from right t left because I am left-handed. I don't care if it's hard for others to read it; maybe I prefer to hav my notes in a sort of secret code for now. But one day I will mak a collection of my notes, a treatise on painting, perhaps, and if I cannot finish it, one of my students will. Eventually I would like everyone to be able t read, understand, and use my studies of painting and the anatomy of people and animals, of the construction of machines, of the way we should live and ea (I've become a vegetarian), and so much more. I have lived in ar extraordinary period, during which I have imagined and created extraordinary things

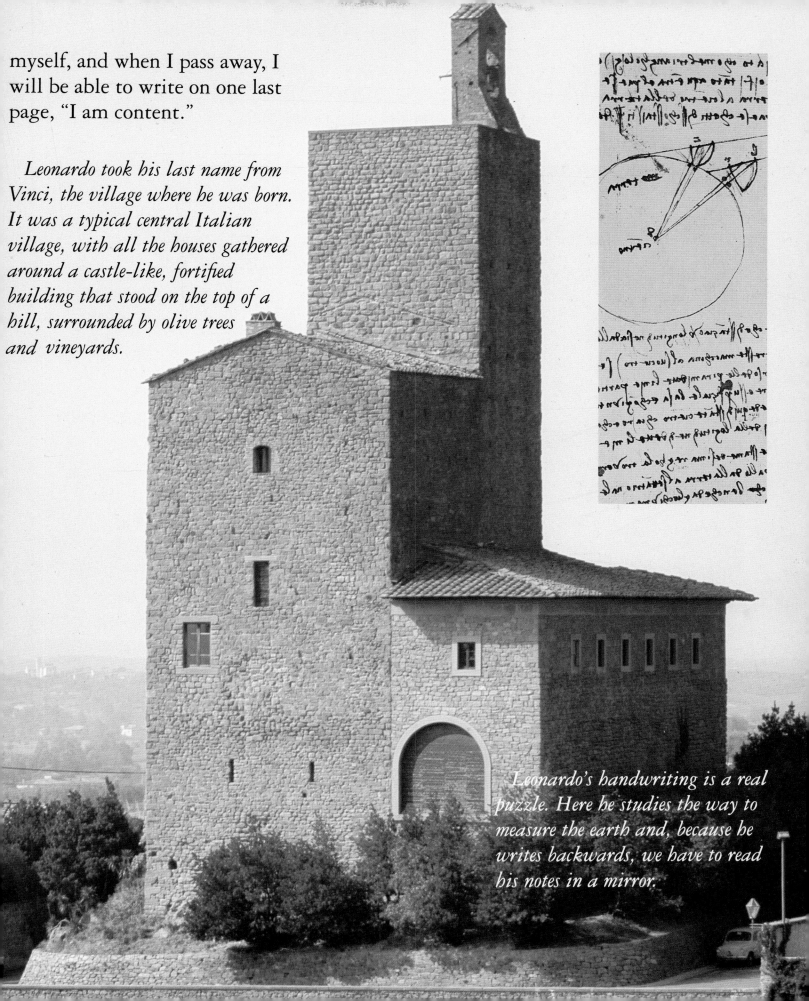

myself, and when I pass away, I will be able to write on one last page, "I am content."

*Leonardo took his last name from Vinci, the village where he was born. It was a typical central Italian village, with all the houses gathered around a castle-like, fortified building that stood on the top of a hill, surrounded by olive trees and vineyards.*

*Leonardo's handwriting is a real puzzle. Here he studies the way to measure the earth and, because he writes backwards, we have to read his notes in a mirror.*

In the early part of the new century, towards 1516, when I left Italy to go and live at the manor in Clos-Lucé at the invitation of the king of France, I was already famous. And now I am a well-respected man, but there was a time when people called me eccentric, or even bizarre. They said that I was always

ready to make fun of people, that I was even rude at times. Do you think they were just jealous of me? When I left my tiny hometown at the age of seventeen and my father sent me to be an apprentice to a well-known artist in the city of Florence, someone wrote that I was a "handsome, graceful, and good-looking" young man. Later, though, I shocked some people with my independence; they even criticized the way I dressed because I wore "a rose-colored garment that fell {only} as far as the knees," whereas the fashion of the day called for long robes. Well, what is wrong with being different? I have an adventurous spirit, somewhat rebellious too, that has annoyed many people, I'm afraid. While some artists are happy to repeat what others have done before them, I always want to try something new. And, in fact, I believe that is why I have come to be admired.

*From the window of his room in Clos-Lucé in the valley of the Loire River in central France, Leonardo could see the Royal Palace of Amboise. You can see the drawing he made, on the left-hand page, probably of this view. King Francis I, whose portrait by the French painter Jean Clouet is on the opposite page, was a great ruler of France. He invited many brilliant scholars and artists of genius from all parts of Europe, and particularly from Italy, to his court.*

When I was about twenty-nine years old and still living in Florence, Italy, the monks of an important church asked me to paint the three kings presenting their gifts to the Christ Child. This scene, *The Adoration of the Magi,* is a subject that many others had painted before me, always in the same way, as a happy, touching story filled with hope. I wanted, instead, to show it as the powerful event it must really have been—an overwhelming event that makes horses rear in fright, old men bow to the ground, and others gesture dramatically. Everyone is awed and a little frightened by this unknown child who will change the course of history. The contract said I should "finish" this painting in twenty-four or thirty months at the latest. Tell me, though, how could I "finish" or "put the finishing touches" on an event that has no end? Everyone said that I ran away from Florence without finishing the painting. You can judge for yourself if this is true. Look at this picture (on the opposite page) of the painting just as I left it. For contrast, I show it to you with one of my first drawings, a sketch of a lovely Tuscan valley. (I think it is the *Valley of the Arno*—the beautiful river that flows through Florence, but I'm not sure; it was a long time ago when I made this sketch, and I don't remember.)

Anyway, I did the painting the way I wanted to, and caused problems. Sometimes, however, fate seemed to be working against me. For instance, not so long ago I was asked to paint a picture in *fresco* (that is, instead of painting with oil paints on canvas I used watercolors directly on fresh wet plaster) on one wall of a hall in the *Palazzo Vecchio,* or Old Palace in Florence. I was to show the struggle for the standard, or flag, during the *Battle of Anghiari,* which the Florentines had just won against the duke of the rival city of Milan. I was very enthusiastic about the subject. It called for a great many different figures with a wide variety of expressions. I would have to give "dynamic forms to the different bodies," showing a tumultuous clash of horses and men in a scene charged with emotion. In short, it was a painting that would give my lively imagination plenty to do and the job was an important one, too. First I made the "cartoon," which in this sort of work is the paper sketch from which you transfer your drawing of the subject, enlarged to the proper size, onto the wall. In this case, the wall was more than fifty feet long! Then, everything started to go wrong. Michelangelo, a young artist whom I do not like at all, was invited to decorate the opposite wall of the hall and to paint another battle scene there.

Next, and I'll read you my notes from Friday, June 6, 1505, "Just as I was applying the first brushstroke, the weather changed for the worse: an alarm was rung to call the townspeople together. The cartoon was torn and water spilled all over it, for a vessel someone had been carrying broke. The weather having abruptly changed, there followed a great downpour of rain until evening, with day as dark as night." All my work was flooded, washed off, destroyed, and I was so upset that I never went back to that painting again.

Well, before coming to France, I lived in Milan, Italy, for nearly seventeen years, between 1453 and 1500. There I did many works, not just paintings but also designs for new kinds of weapons and other useful machines, mainly for Duke Ludovico Sforza. The duke was about my age and was called "the Moor," probably because of his dark hair and deeply tanned skin. The name Sforza, too, is a kind of nickname, first given to one of his ancestors who was said to be as strong as Hercules and who was able to force (*sforzare* in Italian) his way past any obstacle. And Ludovico himself also had a very strong will. From Florence I had sent him a letter in which I told him about all the clever devices, engines, and machines I had designed to help him win battles or lay siege to a city. I invented very handy bombards (early cannons), completely silent mines with hidden tubes, and all sorts of other weapons, each new one more fearful than the one before it.

*During his lifetime, there were many wars, and Leonardo was often asked to design weapons. For defending a fort, he imagined this bombard, which looks like a fireworks display or a series of fountains.*

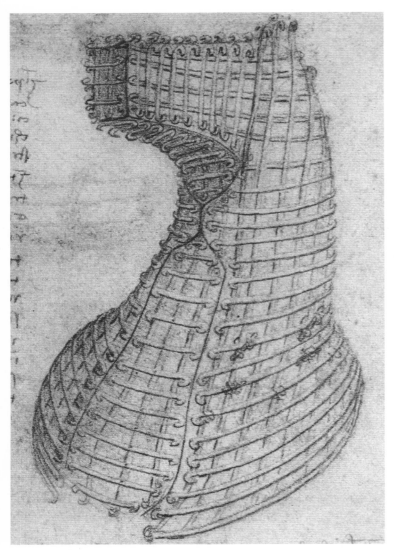

I then wrote to him that "I can also take charge of creating a bronze horse that will be an immortal honor and eternal monument to your renowned father and the illustrious house of Sforza." Ludovico did, in fact, give me the job of making this statue. So I moved to Milan in 1483. Little did I imagine that this work would keep me busy there for more than sixteen years! I wanted to create something that had never been done before—a statue of a man riding a horse that is rearing up on its hind legs. The problem was how to keep the whole thing from toppling over. How do you hold up an unsteady horse over twenty-three feet high? The whole work, with base and rider, was to be nearly forty-six feet high, and I would need seventy-two tons of bronze to make it. I did a lot of research first, making sketches, more and more detailed drawings, and above all, studies of horses from life. I often went to the duke's stables, where I would look carefully at the muscle structure and behavior of the horses. I was quite upset by the condition of the stables. I wrote that they should be "clean and in order, unlike current practices." Thus, I imagined all kinds of systems, such as troughs that would fill automatically, to improve these animals' living conditions. But, in spite of all these distractions, I completed the clay model of the statue and in November 1493 unveiled it before the Palace. I was right to be proud. The statue's breathless, impetuous aspect earned it great praise from everyone. All that I had left to do was to cast the statue in bronze. To solve all the problems connected with this took a great deal of my time and cleverness. I turned my attention to making the mold for shaping the huge metal figure, and building the frame to hold the white-hot molten bronze. Finally all my plans were perfect and I was ready to go ahead—but just then Ludovico Sforza and the people of Milan were having some troubles; in 1494 the French armies entered Italy, more or less with Ludovico's consent. And before long, the seventy-two tons of bronze that had been set aside for my statue were loaded onto a ship bound for Genoa to be made into cannons. The clay model standing in the square before the Palace gradually crumbled away until nothing was left of it.

*The fate of the equestrian monument designed by Leonardo in praise of Ludovico the Moor's father is seen between these illustrations. The left-hand page shows the outline of the* Framework of the Mold *in which the horse's head was to be cast. On the right is seen a drawing of a* Cannon Foundry.

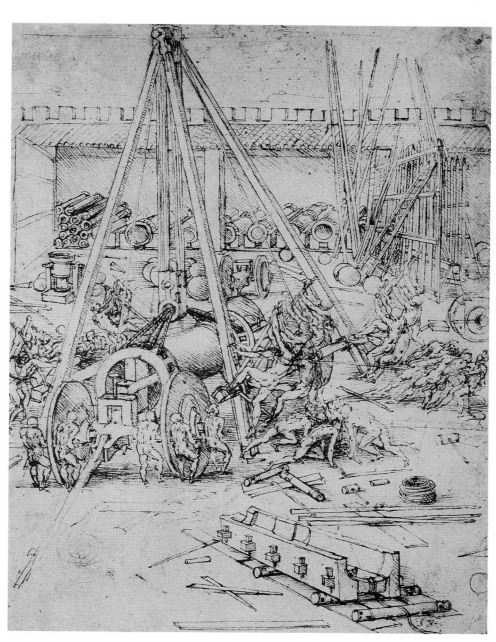

During the time that I was working in Milan, people said that I was living in great style. It's true, I had many servants, apprentices, and more or less qualified assistants. I also owned all kinds of animals which I took care of with great patience. Even before that, when I lived in Florence, I had owned many horses which I loved to train, and I also had a lot of cats. I have drawn them so many times! Cats are marvelous to draw when they are sleeping all rolled up into a ball, or washing themselves, or when they bristle and arch their backs. I have observed horses, too, and drawn them, of course. It is fascinating to see how easily, with just a few alterations, you can transform a horse's muzzle into the head of a man! And if you want to make a fantastic animal, a dragon for example, I'll give you the recipe. Take the head of a large hound, a mastiff or pointer,

the eyes of a cat, the ears of a porcupine, the snout of a greyhound, the eyebrows of a lion, the forehead of an old rooster, and the neck of a turtle. You can't miss. But do you think I am just playing? Not exactly—I have always taken great pleasure in prying into all of nature's secrets and learning about every field of knowledge.

23

*The Sforzas' castle in Milan. Turrets and towers, the whole impression of a fortress, revealed in a few strokes of Leonardo's pen. Drawing in perspective, that is, showing some things close up and others far away, was one of the great discoveries of the Renaissance. Leonardo used geometry to figure out the exact proportions of objects or people he drew.*

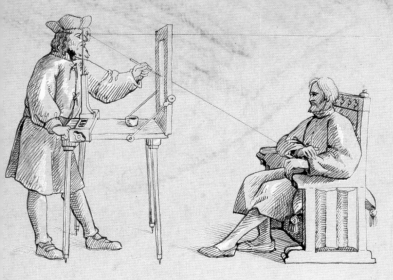

Because of the work I had to do in Milan, I realized I needed a real studio. I have made some notes about what would be the ideal studio for me. I would choose one with small rooms because they arouse the mind, whereas large ones lead it astray. It would have big windows fitted with movable screens that could be raised or lowered according to the amount of light needed for what I was working on, and a system of pulleys that would allow me to adjust the height of my work table. Of course, some of this was just in my imagination but soon I had my studio comfortably set up and I felt ready to take on even the most difficult jobs. I love the challenge of finding new solutions to problems. Nothing escapes my curiosity and above all my thirst for scientific knowledge, for science is the captain, practice the soldier. It was with confidence therefore that I took on the most difficult jobs, dreaming up new and original ways to get them done.

This is one of the reasons why I pondered quite a long time about just how I should show the scene from the Bible of *The Last Supper*. I had been hired to decorate the refectory, or dining hall, of the Convent of Santa Maria delle Grazie in Milan. Before painting the disciples at Christ's last meal, I had studied each reaction, attitude, grimace, and gesture. I had observed real people carefully in the unlikeliest, even the most disreputable places imaginable. The wall I was to paint was damp, the refectory itself poorly ventilated. I painted it so quickly, from 1495 to 1497, that some people might think I used oils, but it was all in fresco, on plaster. I knew this work was fragile, but it was perfectly painted. How long will it last, I wonder? Must everything I do end up falling apart and disappearing? Not always, fortunately. In Milan, I also did several striking pictures on wood, a new kind of painting at that time. And now, King Francis I and his court admire my paintings greatly and I still like to look at those I've brought with me here to France. That trip from Italy to France was some expedition, believe me! But I will tell you about that later. Now I want to talk to you about what I call my "trifles."

The Last Supper *is one of Leonardo's most famous works. He painted it on a large wall, about twenty-eight feet long and thirteen and one-half feet high. Unfortunately, this work had already begun to show signs of deteriorating in the painter's lifetime, and has often had to be restored since then. Before deciding on this composition, Leonardo drew several others which reveal all the solutions he thought of to the problem of showing a panoramic view of the disciples around the table.*

I have always been a great creator and director of spectacles, balls, pageants, parades, cavalcades, and so on. But what remains of all that? Alas, nothing. But I was happy to create a fleeting moment of joy and splendor for the delight of all, after which, indeed, nothing remained. The Medicis, the princes who ruled Florence, loved to host lavish celebrations. The city lived "blissfully, in the exhilaration of jousting tournaments, triumphal processions, and feasts public and private," wrote one poet. And naturally I was glad to take part in the merrymaking. Later, in Milan, under Ludovico Sforza, the celebrations would continue with festival after festival, as lavish as the payments I got for my work. Perhaps Ludovico and others were hoping to make everyone forget those sad years when the plague had ravaged the city, from 1484 to 1486.

*Tournaments, bull races, and naval battles were held in a stadium, just as they had been long ago in ancient Rome. Public celebrations grew in number throughout the sixteenth century. On the opposite page a French engraver depicts a* Tournament *held in 1565 in the Belvedere courtyard of the Vatican in Rome. An immense stairway ran between two platforms, and spectators were seated on rows of benches in the center, on the side porticoes, and even on the sills of the Palace windows.*

On January 13, 1490 the Feast of Paradise, also known as the Ball of the Planets, began, and I was the grand organizer of this public celebration. The Feast was a huge success. People said that I was "the marvelous creator and judge of the ornaments and above all of the most amusing spectacles." The theme of the spectacles had been set by the duke himself with the help of his astrologer. The festivities began with dances, then a parade complete with marvelous costumes and masks, followed by a cavalcade with those on horseback dressed as "wildmen." There was music, too—harmonious sounds coming from various instruments I had designed myself. But the most wonderful part came at midnight when, as the music fell silent and a dome of greenery hid the ceiling of the hall, a curtain was drawn back. One dazzled witness wrote that there then appeared "the vault of heaven, in motion thanks to a semi-circular mechanism built with iron rings, and a series of lights hanging from seven children who shone as brightly as the seven planets themselves." And the ambassador from the city of Ferrara added that "behind a window, illuminated by torches, stood the twelve signs of the zodiac, offering a marvelous spectacle." The following year there was a splendid feast as well as a great tournament to celebrate Ludovico Sforza's marriage to Beatrice d'Este. Engaged at the age of five, married to the duke at fifteen, Beatrice was very beautiful, a strong-willed and charming young woman.

*On May 25, 1517, when the king of France, Louis XII, made his entry into Milan, the city built three triumphal arches in his honor, while two hundred young people dressed in blue satin were on hand to welcome him. Here is the drawing Leonardo made of one of their costumes (opposite); he also drew these* Maidens Dancing with Their Veils to the Sound of the Tambourine. *Dancing was, of course, part of every celebration and Leonardo acted as choreographer. He was a musician as well, engineer-musician, we ought to say, for he invented various instruments, like this mechanical drum mounted on a cart. The cart's forward motion worked a crank that in turn beat the drum.*

31

Five years later, in January of 1496, the city was once more the scene of great festivities. These would be the last the duke was to offer to the public. The high point was the spectacle of the story of Danae. Danae was a princess in a Greek myth whose father had locked her in a bronze tower. The god Zeus would come and visit her disguised as golden rain. For this I had made a very complicated device that could raise an actor high in the air, lower him from the ceiling, and also revolve the platform of the stage.

*Very often Leonardo's paintings contain mysteries, as in this* Portrait of a Musician. *Who is the man in the painting? What is the music on the score where we read the letters CANT ANG . . . ? Why are the face and hair carefully done while the chest and hand were left unfinished? On the page facing him is* La Belle Ferronière. *Is this the name of some lady at the court of Francis I, as many people have thought? No, the* ferronière *is a piece of jewelry in the form of a thin ribbon encircling the brow. It was fashionable in Leonardo's day to add a precious stone in the center of the forehead.*

The skill of the actors' performances and the technical feats accomplished by my machinery were sensational. The music too. I myself play what we call in Italian the *lira da braccio*, literally the "arm lyre," and I have a beautiful voice. Staging the play, making the set, scenery, and costumes, calculating the perspective so that a spectator can see as well from far away as close up, all these problems are similar to those that fascinate me when I'm painting, whether in fresco (remember *The Last Supper*), in oil, or even when I'm drawing.

*Leonardo was a musician and played an instrument identical to the one shown here. This is a* lira da braccio, *an ancestor of the violin. It was also played with a bow, but had more strings than a modern violin. Poets used these instruments to accompany themselves while they recited epic works and legends of knights.*

I was still living in Milan when I signed a contract to do a large painting that was planned for a church altar and, therefore, had several parts. I agreed to do the central section while some painter friends I was staying with took care of doing the side panels. The contract described how the work should look down to the smallest detail: the rounded form of the central section; the work's size (it was to be over six feet high); the material the work should be painted on (wood); the setting of the scene; the gilt molding of the frame; the deadline for finishing the painting, which was to be at the end of the year; the total payment each artist would get; and the possibility of appeal if the finished work was not satisfactory. Yet in spite of all this careful planning, there followed a lawsuit that would last close to twenty-five years! True, the suit was just about a question of money—there was never a complaint about the quality of my work.

*This plant is known by the beautiful name* Star of Bethlehem. *With the precision of a botanist, Leonardo drew flowers, plants, and trees. The interest he showed in them was twofold, that of a scientist and that of an artist. With the same spirit of careful observation, he drew his own "weary" left hand (above).*

*On the opposite page is a detail from Leonardo famous painting,* The Virgin of the Rocks. *Look at Mary's face carefully, and notice her expression with its suggestion of mystery and sadness.*

I painted the Virgin Mary, the Christ Child, Saint John the Baptist and an angel, the entire group placed at the mouth of a cave. This painting is called *The Virgin of the Rocks* (although I don't like giving titles to my works). One day, before I did this painting, I was walking in the mountains and I came upon a cave. Here is what I wrote in my notebook about this: "Driven by a burning desire, anxious to see the abundance of strange and varied forms crafty Nature creates, having made my way a certain distance between the overhanging rocks, I arrived at the entrance to a great cave, and paused there a moment astonished, for I had not suspected its existence. With back bent, and gripping my knee with my left hand while I shielded my forehead with the light, I leaned from side to side, knitting my brows and peering to see if I could make out anything inside in spite of the dense shadows that reigned there. After I had remained so for a moment, two emotions arose in me, fear and desire; fear of the dark, menacing cave and desire to discover if it concealed some marvel or other. . . ." These same strange emotions guided my brush when I painted this group of figures before the mouth of a cave. I especially wanted to capture in paint the disturbing play of subtle shades of light and dark; I wanted to show the mysterious grandeur of nature, whether in the beauty of flowers, the dazzle of the sky, or the awesome depths of the "menacing cave."

But little by little, I began to feel threatened by more than just a menacing cave: My life, though I was still filled with passion and enthusiasm, was becoming troubled. Actually, it was more the period I lived in, rather than my life itself, that was troubled. You would have thought that everyone was at war. Ludovico Sforza, my former patron, had been defeated and captured by the French; he died after eight years in prison. In the early years of the new (16th) century, a monk in Florence called Girolamo Savonarola began to foretell the ruin of Italy. An outspoken and fiery reformer, he even criticized me for leading "an existence so unstable, so uncertain that one might say he [speaking of me] lives from day to day!" Tell me, how else could I have lived? I began to work as a military engineer for the powerful Cesare Borgia. Son of a pope and leader of a mercenary army, Cesare was fighting on the side of the king of France, to whom he wanted to offer control of central Italy. Cesare Borgia's craftiness and cruelty are legendary. During the five or six years I was in his service, I was put in charge of canal building. I had many projects; I had to link the city of Florence with the Mediterranean Sea by a canal, divert the Arno river during the the siege of Pisa, and drain the Pontine Marshes near Rome.

Did Leonardo the engineer invent the airplane? Obviously not. Yet he spent much time studying the flight of birds (right) and thought seriously about making the famous "dream of Icarus" come true by finding a way to give man wings. About this sketch (below) he wrote, "If you want to test this wing, build one of a height and length of forty yards, using reeds, string, and paper, and attach it to a base weighing two hundred pounds. Next, rapidly lower the lever as shown in the drawing. If the two-hundred pound base rises before the wing is lowered, the experiment is a success, but do try hard to be quick in your movement. If the experiment fails, don't waste any more of your time on it."

Canals, rivers and marshes . . . I'm always having something to do with water—even though water frightens me so. I will never forget the rain that poured down to ruin my work on *The Battle of Anghiari*. Water, flooding, overflowing, has always been a nightmare for me. "Water wears away mountains, fills valleys; it would reduce the world to a perfect sphere," I once wrote in a notebook and added, picturing to myself the Great Flood, "Then will be seen the dark and cloudy air beaten by contrary winds which swirl with incessant rain mixed with hail, where an infinite number of splintered branches twist entangled among countless leaves. . . ." It is a very long, terrifying text, matching my own terror.

*In a page in his notebook about the movement of water, Leonardo penned this* Silhouette of an Old Man *lost in his thoughts. He probably meant to show himself during his retirement in his house on the banks of the Loire River in France.*

*This admirable portrait (opposite) of a young woman, beautiful, sad, and deathly pale, is another of Leonardo's puzzles. Why does she look so sorrowful? Leonardo himself hated giving his paintings titles, so this painting is known only as the* Portrait of Ginevra Benci, *which does not give us a key to the mystery of her expression.*

I eventually went to live in Rome. I was already an old man by then—and even if I like appearing so, growing old also means being less willing to put up with people. And in Rome I could no longer keep count of my troubles and worries. Although I lived comfortably at the Belvedere, the Vatican's private residence, I received no commissions—no one seemed to want my paintings any more. It was the young artists like Raphael and Michelangelo who were called on to paint. The work begun, according to my ideas, to drain the Pontine Marshes was stopped—I don't know why; I was forbidden to continue my studies in anatomy and dissection that I had been doing at the hospital; my assistants (foreigners who couldn't understand, or pretended not to understand, what I said) were all good-for-nothing idlers, thieves, who gave away my ideas to others. So, tell me, why should I stay where I felt so unwanted?

The Virgin and Child with Saint Anne, Mona Lisa, *and* Saint John the Baptist *are the three paintings Leonardo brought with him when he left Italy for France. The caravan crossed the Alps by way of the Mont-Genèvre pass. Here he drew this fortress-like "rampart" formed by a two-faced mountain called the Janus.*

So, in the fall of the year 1516 I left Italy. What a trip! With a few friends for company, and several pack mules laden with many cases, trunks, and paintings, I set off for the castle of Francis I, the king of France. We traveled by way of Florence and Milan, in Italy, then over the Alps at Mont-Genèvre, and on through the French towns of Grenoble, Lyons, Vierzon and Le Cher, to arrive at last in Amboise, south of Paris in the valley of the Loire River.

So here I am, the old lion, living in the Clos-Lucé, the beautiful royal house next to the king's castle. It's here that I in turn have invited you to spend a weekend with me. I like it here, for I am loved by the king and his court, cared for, and admired. Have I told you that I've brought three of my paintings with me? I think perhaps they are the three most remarkable paintings I've ever done. One is a portrait of a woman—with their strange custom of giving names to works of art, people call this *Mona Lisa* or *La Gioconda*, but no matter—one is a group picture, *The Virgin and Child with Saint Anne*, and finally, my last painting, *Saint John the Baptist*. I want you to take another look at them. Tell me, what do you see there? How are they similar? Each of them looks at you with a kind of smile, a smile you would find difficult to describe. You'll see, you will remember that mysterious smile for a long time; it is a smile that come from the memory of my long life as an artist with an intense curiosity about nature, science, religion, technology—and especially about people.

# TO SEE
# LEONARDO'S WORKS

*Leonardo has just told you the story of his long life, filled with discoveries, taking you with him as he traveled across northern Italy and France during the Renaissance. The works of art which he has shown you along the way can now be found in libraries and museums in these and many other countries. If you wanted to see them all, you would have to take a real world tour. But let us be your guide to some of them, beginning with those in the United States.*

## UNITED STATES
### National Gallery of Art, Washington

The libraries and museums of the United States have collected many marvelous drawings by Leonardo, but they possess only two paintings. The first is the *Portrait Of Ginevra Benci,* also called *The Woman with a Juniper Tree,* which is quite mysterious. Is this the portrait of the young poetess, Ginevra Benci, a banker's daughter much admired by Lorenzo the Magnificent? Or is it a play on words or a pun on the juniper tree, which has given the picture its name? On top of that, Leonardo used of a most unusual technique in this work: he didn't paint it with paintbrushes but, rather, with his fingers—his fingerprints can be found all over it! The National Gallery also has a *Madonna and Child with a Pomegranate* which *may* have been painted by Leonardo, but no one is quite certain.

### New York, The Metropolitan Museum of Art

This enormous museum has several of Leonardo's drawings in the special Robert Wood Johnson gallery for drawings, prints, and photographs. As you read in the story, Leonardo made many notes and sketches for each work that he did, and you will find a few here. They own a *Study for a Nativity,* a drawing of a *Head of a Man in Profile,* another of the *Head of the Virgin,* and a page with some *Designs for a Stage Setting.* In the Robert Lehman Collection of the museum they have another drawing which is of a *Bear Walking.* These drawings are very delicate so they are kept in a special dark room most of the time. You may want to call ahead and find out if they are on display before going to see them.

### New York, The Pierpont Morgan Library

In financier Pierpont Morgan's collection you can see a page of Leonardo's *Designs for Two Machines.*

# Malibu, California, The J. Paul Getty Museum

A visit to this great museum is bound to be a highlight of any trip to this sunny state. Here you can see two pages of drawings by Da Vinci. One of them is double-sided. On the front (called recto) are three sketches of a *Child with a Lamb,* and on the back (verso) you'll see *A Child with a Lamb,* the *Head of an Old Man,* and *Studies for Machinery.* The other has the strange title of *Caricature of a man with bushy hair.*

# FRANCE
## Paris, The Louvre Museum

For lovers of Leonardo, present and future, the Louvre Museum offers a visual feast. The pictures hanging there are the most distinguished of all those that Leonardo painted; they come from the royal collections. *The Virgin of the Rocks* for example, was given to King Francis I as a sort of consolation prize for not having been able to bring *The Last Supper* to France!

Everything concerning Leonardo seems to have something slightly strange and unexpected about it. Thus, there are two versions of *The Virgin of the Rocks.* They are very similar, but not identical—one is at the Louvre and the other is at the National Gallery in London. *La Gioconda* is another mystery painting. This one, attracts more visitors than any other work of art in the museum. But who is the subject of the painting? To an illustrious visitor who came to see him at Clos-Lucé Leonardo said only, as he showed him the painting: "I painted this portrait of a young Florentine woman at the burning request of Giuliano de Medici." People think that this Florentine beauty's name was Mona Lisa.

Among the works of Leonardo we have shown you in the book, you will find these at the Louvre: *The Virgin of the Rocks* (pages 35 and 36–37); *Saint John the Baptist* (page 44); *Mona Lisa* or *La Gioconda* (pages 44 and 47); *The Virgin with the Infant Jesus and Saint Anne* (page 44) and *La Belle Ferronière* (page 33), which Leonardo painted in collaboration with Boltraffio.

The Portrait of Francis I which is reproduced on page 12 is also to be found at the Louvre, but it is not by Leonardo. It ws done by the Frenchman Jean Clouet, painter, miniaturist and extremely fine draftsman who did excellent portraits of all the important people of his time: it is thanks to him that we have a lifelike image of the king who so loved the art of Leonardo.

## Cloux (Clos-Lucé), Leonardo's House

We have mentioned the dwelling at Cloux (Clos-Lucé) where the king of France welcomed Leonardo in the last years of his life, settling him scarcely five hundred yards from his own castle at Amboise. Located in the Loire valley, Clos-Lucé today is a magical place where the atmosphere, and a collection of forty models made from Leonardo's designs allow one to recapture the spirit of his day.

## ITALY
## Florence, Uffizi Museum

Since Leonardo was Italian, and spent most of his life in Italy many of his works remain there. One can only imagine how surprised the commissioners of the painting *The Adoration of the Magi* (page 14, top) must have been when they first saw it, for Leonardo had left it "incompleted." He had painted neither shepherds nor kings, and the barn with the ox and the donkey had disappeared, to be replaced by ruins. The museum also has two splendid *Studies for the Adoration of the Magi* (page 15).

## Milan, Santa Maria delle Grazie

This work reveals the damage that time and poor conservation techniques can wreak, and *The Last Supper* stands as an emblem of the impossible masterpiece. It fascinated the kings of France so much that Francis I wanted to have the wall sawed off so he could take it back with him. It has continued to deteriorate over the centuries—and to be restored—right up to the present day. It is almost the ghost of a painting now, but still it awes us.

## Milan, National Museum of Science and Technology

In this museum, located in a former monastery, the entire first floor is devoted to the research and inventions of Leonardo. And here one can admire magnificent models of some of the machines he designed.

## Milan, Ambrosiana Museum

Here you will see the *Portrait of a Musician* (page 32). This musician is thought to have been the music-master of the chapel of the Duomo (the great cathedral of Milan), who was Leonardo's close friend.

## Turin, The Royal Library

The library of the royal palace in Turin contains the splendid face of an old man, drawn in sanguine (red chalk), which is reproduced on page 6 and which is probably a *Self Portrait*. However, one cannot say this with certainty, for Leonardo was not in the habit of using himself as a model, as so many other artists did. And yet he himself stated that painting was the only way to "conserve the beauty that nature and time rendered fleeting, to conserve the features of famous men."

# ENGLAND
## London, The British Museum

The British Museum is an immense institution, located in the heart of London. Its collection of engravings and drawings is one of the richest in the world and includes, in particular, the preparatory "cartoon" for *Saint John the Baptist*.

## Windsor Castle, Royal Library

The Royal Castle at Windsor, east of London, contains many art treasures. It owns more than six hundred drawings by Leonardo from the royal collections of the seventeenth century, including some which were left by the painter to his disciple Francesco Melzi. Eighteen drawings from this fabulous collection illustrate the main themes of this book (pages 7, 11, 12, 13, 17, 18–19, 21, 22, 23, 24, 29, 30, 40–41, 42, 44–45, and 46).

This is just the beginning of our world tour in search of the works of Leonardo. But you can admire them in many other places, too, in Spain, Austria, and Hungary (the *Head of a Warrior* on page 16 is from the Museum of Fine Arts in Budapest), to name but a few more. It's up to you to find these and others. Enjoy your treasure-hunting!

# PAINTINGS, SKETCHES, DRAWINGS AND EXTRACTS FROM NOTEBOOKS REPRODUCED IN THIS BOOK

*The list that follows gives the titles and media of the works reproduced as well as the places where they can be found. The dimensions are given, by height and width, expressed in centimeters. Unless otherwise indicated, photographs are archival documents.*

## Page 5
*How to walk on water.* Pen and ink. From the Codex Atlanticus 7 r-a. Milan, Ambrosiana Museum.

## Page 6
*Self-portrait (?),* c. 1503. Sanguine on yellowed white paper, oxidation spots, 33.3 x 21.3 cm. Turin, Royal Library.

## Page 7
*Hand of the angel Gabriel,* study for *The Virgin of the Rocks,* c. 1483. Windsor Castle, Royal Library.

Masks with lions' heads, perhaps for the tournament at the wedding of Ludovico Sforza, "the Moor," Milan, 1491. Windsor Castle, Royal Library.

## Page 8
*Lion roaring,* drawing attributed to Leonardo. Paris, Louvre Museum.

## Page 9
*Saint John the Baptist,* detail of *The Infant Jesus, the Virgin, Saint Anne and Saint John the Baptist.* 1499–1500. Preparatory cartoon, charcoal. London, British Museum.

## Pages 10–11
View of the village of Vinci (Tuscany) with the dungeon. Recent photograph courtesy of Scala, Florence.

## Page 11
Writing by Leonardo. Page of a study for measuring the earth from the surface to the center. Windsor Castle, Royal Library.

## Page 12
*Amboise Castle seen from the window of Leonardo's bedroom at Cloux* (Clos-Lucé). Drawing attributed to Leonardo. Red chalk on white paper, 13.3 x 26.3 cm. Windsor Castle, Royal Library.

Jean Clouet (1485/90–1540/41). *Francis I*, detail, c. 1520–25. 96 x 74 cm. Paris, Louvre Museum. Photograph courtesy of RMN, Paris.

## Page 13
*Horse,* study for *The Battle of Anghiari.* c. 1504. Drawing. Windsor Castle, Royal Library.

## Page 14
Two studies for *The Adoration of the Magi.* Florence, Uffizi Museum. Photograph courtesy of Scala, Florence.

## Page 15
*The Adoration of the Magi* (unfinished), 1481–82. Oil on wood, 246 x 243 cm. Florence, Uffizi Museum. Photograph courtesy of Scala, Florence.

*View of the Arno Valley,* dated "The Day of the Holy Virgin of the Snows, August 2, 1483." Pen and ink. Florence, Uffizi Museum. Photograph courtesy of Scala, Florence.

## Page 16
*Head of a soldier,* study for *The Battle of Anghiari,* 1503–05. Black chalk. Budapest, Fine Arts Museum.

## Page 17
*Horse whinnying,* study for *The Battle of Anghiari,* c. 1504. Sanguine, 15.3 x 14.2 cm., Windsor Castle, Royal Library.

## Pages 18–19
Plan for defense of fortifications with "fountains" of bombs. Pen and brown ink, 32.9 x 48 cm. Windsor Castle, Royal Library.

## Page 20
Plan of metal armature for the casting mold of the Sforza Horse. Madrid, National Library.

## Page 21
*Courtyard of a cannon foundry,* c. 1487. Silverpoint enhanced with pen on brown paper, 25 x 18.3 cm. Windsor Castle, Royal Library.

## Page 22
*Horses, lion's head, figure of a man,* study for *The Battle of Anghiari,* c. 1504. Pen and ink, 19.6 x 30.8 cm. Windsor Castle, Royal Library.

## Pages 22–23
*Studies of cats,* c. 1506. Black chalk enhanced with pen and ink. Windsor Castle, Royal Library.

## Page 33

In collaboration with Boltraffio (1467–1516): *The Beautiful Ferronnière,* c. 1485–88. On wood. 62 x 44 cm. Paris, Louvre Museum. Photograph courtesy of Scala, Florence.

## Page 34

Hand of Leonardo drawing, generally called *The Tired Hand*. Pen. From the Codex Atlanticus 283 v-b. Milan, Ambrosiana Museum.

Plant study of the Star of Bethlehem. Photograph courtesy of Scala, Florence.

## Page 35

*Figure of the Virgin,* detail of *The Virgin of the Rocks*, 1483–90. Paris, Louvre Museum. Photograph courtesy of Scala, Florence.

## Page 36

*The Virgin of the Rocks*, 1483–90. 198 x 123 cm. Paris, Louvre Museum. Photograph courtesy of Scala, Florence.

## Pages 36–37

*The grotto,* detail of *The Virgin of the Rocks*, 1483–90. Paris, Louvre Museum. Photograph courtesy of Scala, Florence.

## Pages 38–39

Experimental design for a wing from *Ornitottero* (flying man). Drawing. Paris, French Institute. Ms B f.88v.

## Page 39

Systematic study of the flight of birds. Drawing. From the Codex Volo Uccelli f.8r. Turin, Royal Library. Photograph courtesy of Scala, Florence.

## Pages 40–41

*The Flood, with Neptune and the gods of the winds,* c. 1514. Black chalk enhanced with pen on gray paper, 27 x 40.8 cm. Windsor Castle, Royal Library.

## Page 42

*Old man, meditating,* left side of page, c. 1510. Pen, 15.2 x 10.7 cm. Windsor Castle, Royal Library.

## Page 43

*Portrait of Ginevra Benci (?)* or *Portrait of a Woman with a Juniper Tree,* c. 1474. On wood, 42 x 37 cm. Washington D.C., National Gallery of Art.

## Page 44
By Leonardo and his pupils: *The Virgin, the Infant Jesus and Saint Anne* (unfinished), c. 1506–10. On wood, 170 x 129 cm. Paris, Louvre Museum. Photograph courtesy of Scala, Florence.

*Mona Lisa* or *La Gioconda*, 1503–05. On wood, 77 x 53. Paris, Louvre Museum. Photograph courtesy of Scala, Florence.

*Saint John the Baptist*, 1513–16. On wood, 69 x 57 cm. Paris, Louvre Museum. Photograph courtesy of Scala, Florence.

## Pages 44–45
*Landscape.* Sanguine on white paper, 9.3 x 15.2 cm. Windsor Castle, Royal Library.

## Page 46
*Dragon.* Pen and pencil, 16 x 24.4 cm. Windsor Castle, Royal Library.

## Page 47
*Mona Lisa* or *La Gioconda*, detail, 1503–05. On wood. Paris, Louvre Museum. Photograph courtesy of Scala, Florence.

## Pages 48–49
Lenten Season in Paris, 1912. La Gioconda's carriage passing in front of the Hotel de Ville (an allusion to the theft of the *Mona Lisa* in 1911). Photograph © Harlingue-Viollet, Paris.

# IMPORTANT DATES IN THE LIFE OF LEONARDO

1452    Leonardo born on April 25 in Vinci (about 46 kilometers southwest of Florence), from which he got his surname.

1472    He joins the Painters' Guild of Florence.

1472-    He enters the studio of the painter and sculptor Verrochio.
1473

1478    First personal commission.

1481    The Church of San Donato in Scopeto, commissions *The Adoration of the Magi* from him.

1482    Moves to Milan to work on the equestrian statue ordered by Count Ludovico ("the Moor") Sforza.

1483    *The Virgin of the Rocks* is ordered by the Brothers of the Conception, a Franciscan order.

1489    Studies in anatomy and architecture.

1490    Giacomo, nicknamed Salai, "came to live with me . . . he is ten years old." Despite his "thieving, lying, stubborn, greedy nature" Leonardo kept him at his side until his death.

1495    Begins work on *The Last Supper* in the refectory of Santa Maria delle Grazie.

1496    Illustrates Pacioli's book *De Divina Proportione* with *The Measurements of the Body*.

1498    Decorates the Sala delle Asse in the Sforzas' castle in Milan. Attempts a flying machine.

1499    Milan is occupied by the French.

1500    The monks of the Annunciation in Florence commission *The Virgin, the Christ Child and Saint Anne* for which he did the cartoon. The picture was painted in 1510.

1502    Leonardo is named as architect and chief engineer of the armies in the service of Cesare Borgia in his campaign in central Italy.

1503    The siege of Pisa. The fresco of *The Battle of Anghiari* is ordered for the Palazzo Vecchio (Old Palace) in Florence.

1504    Leonardo's father dies. Leonardo undertakes the fortification of Piombino and several hydraulic projects.

1503–   Leonardo paints *Mona Lisa*, also called *La Gioconda*.
1507

1506    Leonardo is invited to Milan by the French Governor, Charles d'Amboise.

1507–   He is appointed painter and engineer to Louis XII. Studies in
1508    anatomy and hydraulics.

1513    Leonardo moves to the Belvedere Palace in the Vatican in Rome. Does mathematical research on quadrating the circle and on curved surfaces.

1514    Probably painted *Saint John the Baptist* in this period.

1516    Leaves Italy for France at the invitation of King Francis I.

1517    Moves to Cloux (Clos-Lucé), near Amboise, with Salai and a
        pupil named Francesco Melzi.

1519    On May 2, Leonardo da Vinci dies, having drawn up a will
        naming Melzi as heir to all his manuscripts. Melzi conserves
        these and collects them for publication.

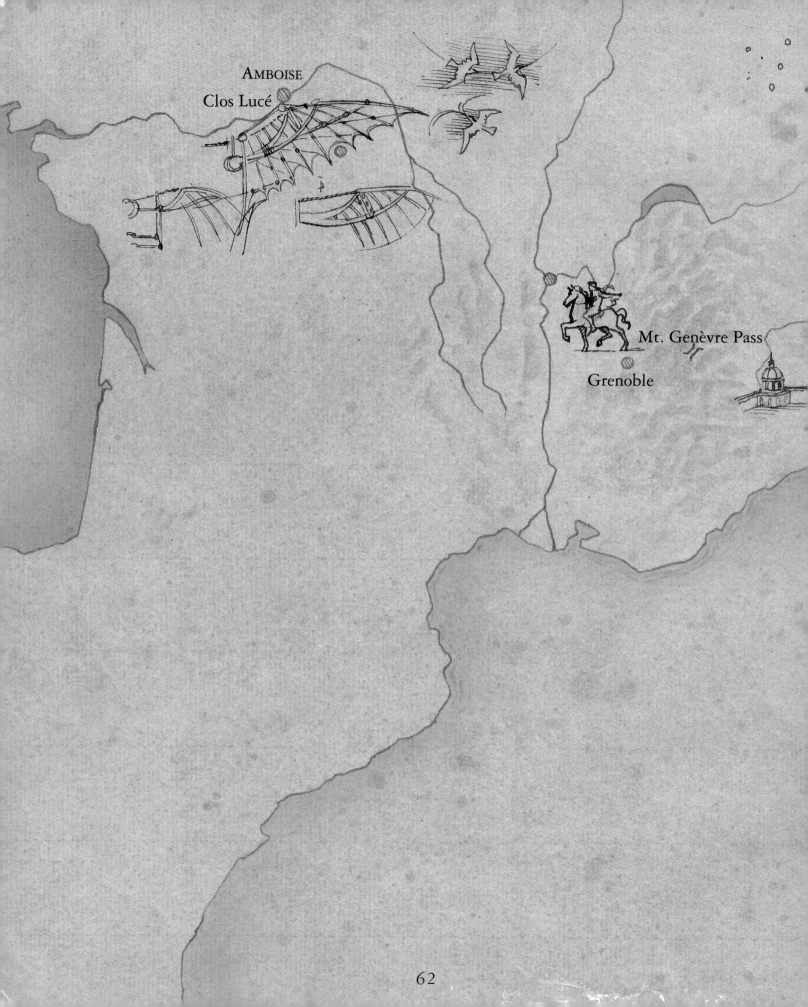

AMBOISE

Clos Lucé

Mt. Genèvre Pass

Grenoble

chiavenna

Valtellina

AN

Parma

Pisa

Piombino

Friuli

Venice

Mantua

Romagne

Vɪɴᴄɪ   Florence

Rome

Map drawn by Pierre-Marie Valat

Other books in this series:

A Weekend with . . .
Velàzquez
Rembrandt
Degas
Renoir
Picasso